THE HISTORY OF THE KOREAN WAR: A FASCINATING HISTORICAL GUIDE

By

NICHOLAS PHILLIPS

TABLE OF CONTENTS

Introduction

No war is fought solely on the ground between men with rifles. In each case there are forces moving above and beyond their sight: governments, leaders with axes to grind, ideologies, groups and races who believe that their way must be the correct way, or perhaps a homeland simply wishing to maintain its way of life.

The Korean War (1950-1953) was a bloody and frustrating conflict that arose in the midst of, and because of, a growing ideological battle between communism and capitalism, but also at a time when the United States as a people had little interest in rallying behind yet another war. We had just finished World War II five years earlier, sacrificing at almost every level even while keeping morale high. To put it in simple terms, the Korean War was not popular. Understanding the purpose of the fighting was difficult, even at the time and even to the soldiers on the ground, beyond a general terror that the Commies were coming to get us all. After an initial year of furious activity, the war dragged on for another two with no end in sight and no discernable gains made. As for morale support, or enthusiasm for the cause among the American public, consider the Korean War to have the same trouble as a person with a birthday one month after Christmas. Everyone is tired of shopping and traveling, nobody has any money left, and the weather is worse.

Many years later, the war in Vietnam caught the public attention in a way the Korean War never could. Baby boomers who had been too young to understand or respond to the Korean War were now young adults who could be drafted, who could rebel against their parents, and who could (and did) question their government's actions. Now in the year 2020, people over a certain age mostly know the Korean War through episodes of *M*A*S*H* and those under that age likely know nothing about it beyond a history book chapter they never got around to reading. Just out of curiosity, we searched Wikipedia for lists of films based on wars. The films pertaining to World War II were simply too numerous to count, whereas the Korean War currently has a list of 77 films (about a third of which were made in South Korea). As a base of comparison, the Vietnam War has a list of 186 films, despite it being almost twenty years more recent. The Korean War is not unknown, but it seems unable to capture human interest in quite the way that the wars just before and after it could.

The Korean War is a conflict of layers, taking place on a highly contested piece of Earth, a peninsula jutting off Asia in a primarily terrible spot: directly between the countries of Japan and China, which have for centuries lived in mutual animosity. The purpose behind the conflict was ostensibly to create a united country, while superpowers of the world maneuvered in the background to ensure that the united country would take the shape that best suited their own purposes. Roles changed from the established allies of World War II, suspicions ran wild, and the battle of communism versus capitalism raged in the minds of the superpowers while, somewhere down on the Korean soil, men with rifles fought from holes dug in the ground.

Helpful Things
to Know Before We Go

The Red Scare: Why were we so afraid?

A video series entitled *Visions of War: The Korean War* (2019) was an invaluable resource in compiling this overview. What is remarkable about the series is that it contains not modern analysis, or study blessed with the benefit of hindsight, but 31 episodes of footage and programming that was more or less contemporaneous with the Korean War and its immediate aftermath. Most of the footage was filmed by U.S. Army cameramen. The narration of the films, and distinguished guests of programs such as "The Big Picture," make no attempts at political correctness when they discuss the "Commies," the "Reds" or what they assume is the nature of the Chinese as a people (using adjectives such as *double-talking, sheepish* and *sly*). Chinese POWs are called cowardly for surrendering. Military historian General S.L.A. Marshall frankly calls the Chinese "masters of concealment and deception" and implies that they do not fight fair, although what he is describing is the perfectly sound military maneuver of moving troops at night to avoid being bombed. If American troops did the same, one could easily assume General Marshall would find the action clever and resourceful. In another episode, a soldier's story begins with describing the weather in North Korea as "cold as the heart of a Commie."

Such outright belligerence is not surprising, and it was doubtless returned in kind by the Communist propaganda machine, but what does it mean?

Beginning in the late 1940s, the American people were repeatedly shocked by events we previously thought impossible. In the wake of World War II, several countries were divided and left in the trusteeship of the United States and the Soviet Union, and repeatedly these countries became sharply divided by ideology rather than achieving reunification. The Iron Curtain fell around Eastern Europe and the Soviet Union - formerly our ally - began testing nuclear weapons. We were no longer the only nation with nuclear capabilities. Instances of Soviet espionage came to light, including the highly publicized trial of Ethel and Julius Rosenberg accused of spying for the Soviet Union, who were executed in 1951 for their crimes against the United States. Ever more evidence came to light that the Soviet Union had infiltrated the United States during and after World War II. In China, a civil war flared and was won by the Communist party, leaving two world superpowers in Communist hands.

The House Un-American Activities Committee (formed in 1938) and Senator Joseph McCarthy (operating almost alongside the timeline of the Korean War in his accusations of communist activity) did much to alarm the American public about the Communist threat, using the adage of "Reds" or "Commies" to generally represent any bogeyman that did not promote United States democracy as the best and only way of life. His scare campaign went to extreme lengths, focusing on celebrities and high-ranking officials in his quest to seek out traitors with communist agendas. Red Menace propaganda was distributed advising citizens to report communist activities and turn in their "fishy friends." Sensationalist films like *The Red Menace, My Son John* and *Undercover Spy* helped feed the furor.

The Korean War is considered an ideological war, meaning that the major thrust of the conflict seemed to be about ideas rather than the destruction of an enemy. Ideological wars operate on fear and propaganda, fanning the flames of hatred, suspicion and racism. Ideological wars are also the powder-keg setup for physical wars. As both sides fear the other, weapons and armies are stockpiled in preparation for an attack that might come at any moment. Fears increase as both sides realize the power of the other and a vicious cycle of expensive, frightening preparation goes on.

Both North and South Korea had a system of government that believed itself to be the correct one, and both sides wished to unite Korea under that respective type of government. But neither North nor South was alone in its fight. Both had superpowers backing their ideologies and said superpowers willing to fight indefinitely on soil that was not their own. This conflict of ideology resulted in a war that, ultimately, accomplished little more than the physical destruction of a country and setting a precedent for many proxy wars to come.

Who was involved? Important Names in the Korean Conflict

Before we begin our overview of the war, let's familiarize ourselves with some of the players. This is not a complete list, of course, because the complete roster of those who planned and fought in the Korean War would require a far larger volume of work than this one. The following persons will frequently be referenced:

United States President Harry S. Truman (until 1952). Vice President Truman took over the Presidency upon the death of President Franklin D. Roosevelt. President Truman closed out World War II with the dropping of two atomic bombs on Japan, a controversial act that is nevertheless generally believed to have been a decision that saved countless lives by ending World War II early. Truman was integral in convincing the United Nations to fight against the North Korean Invasion of South Korea.

United States President Dwight D. Eisenhower (elected in 1952). Part of Eisenhower's campaign strategy was to oppose Truman's policies in Korea, although he had been involved in forming them. He portrayed himself as willing to fight Communism by peaceful means. This may seem to be diametrically opposed to the original, national sentiment of "fighting the commies" and winning at all costs. By the time Eisenhower took charge, however, the Korean conflict had become a see-saw of attrition with no end or satisfactory options for victory in sight.

The United Nations. This was a representative group of countries formed after World War II, with the aim of preventing future wars. When North Korea invaded South Korea, it was the United Nations that criticized the attack and agreed that countermeasures should be taken. Eventually 22 United Nations members would send troops to aid the South Korean cause.

General Douglas MacArthur. The Supreme Commander of Allied Forces in the South Pacific in World War II who was still stationed in Japan when the Korean War broke out, and from there was appointed and served Commander-in-Chief of the United Nations forces until he was relieved from duty by President Truman. He was replaced by **General Matthew Ridgway,** in command of the U.S. Eighth Army, who is largely credited with salvaging the Korean War when it seemed Chinese forces would overtake the peninsula.

Kim Il-Sung became Leader of the Democratic People's Republic of Korea (the government established in North Korea). He was put into power by the Soviet Union.

Syngman Rhee was elected president of the Republic of Korea (the government established in South Korea). Some feel he was specifically selected by the United States and heavily promoted as president because of his resistance to communism. His reputation was that of a violent and vindictive leader.

We'll be frequently referring to armies with acronyms. These are:

ROK: The Republic of Korea's Army. This is the South Korean force, which was joined and supported by U.N. Forces.

KPA: The Korean People's Army. This is the North Korean force, which was joined and supported by the People's Volunteer Army of China.

PVA: The People's Volunteer Army of China, which involved themselves directly in the conflict after it seemed that the U.N. Forces were closing in on China.

U.N. Forces: Troops supplied by the 22 countries of the United Nations to stop the Communist aggression. This includes the United States' military forces. Occasionally the United States military acted first or alone, and we'll distinguish the difference when that occurs.

Where did it happen? Areas of Importance in the Korean Conflict

To better understand the strategies employed by both sides of the war, following is a list of important places in Korea. Like the previous list, it is by no means a complete listing of the complex movements of the conflict.

The **Korean peninsula** extends from the southeastern corner of China, with the Yellow Sea to its West and the Japan Sea to its east. A relatively short distance across the Japan Sea lies the island country of Japan.

Japan and its capital city of Tokyo were headquarters for United Nations Strategic Command. At the start of the Korean War, General Douglas MacArthur, Commander of the U.N. forces, was stationed there, as was the 24th Infantry Division. Hundreds of U.S. B26 bombing missions were flown from Japan to lay waste to North Korea.

At the north end of Korea is the **Yalu River,** the border between Korea and Manchurian **China.** This border will be a hot spot in the Korean War, the "do not cross" line, at the peril of turning the war from a Korean conflict into World War III. This was a strong point of contention between General MacArthur and President Truman. Crossing the Yalu River means entering China with a hostile force, basically an act of war against a superpower that also had the backing of the Soviet Union.

The **38th Parallel** is literally the 38 degrees north latitude marker that surrounds the globe for mapping purposes. The 38th Parallel roughly divides the Korean peninsula in half, so was used after World War II to demarcate the line between the northern and southern regions of the country.

The capital cities of North and South Korea, **Pyongyang** and **Seoul,** respectively, are both situated in the middle, western section of the peninsula. Seoul is quite close to and south of the 38th Parallel, whereas Pyongyang is a fair distance north of it.

Port cities you should know:

Incheon (sometimes spelled *Inchon*) is the port city that serves Seoul, as Seoul is approximately twenty miles inland from the coast.

Pusan is a port city in the far southeastern end of Korea and it is heavily utilized by the U.N. Forces to bring in troops and supplies. At one point in the war, the entirety of the U.N. Forces desperately but determinedly held onto a 120-mile beachhead perimeter around Pusan. This area was particularly defensible because of the **Nakdong River,** which basically surrounded it. It was, in dramatic but honest terms, a "last stand" position. The loss of Pusan would have meant the loss of the entire war for the United Nations.

Hungnam is a port city on the eastern side of Korea. It was at this port that U.N. Forces performed a massive evacuation of men, materials and refugees after the Chinese army (the PVA) attacked in North Korea.

Why did it happen? A brief history of Korea

Korea already had a complex history of rule prior to World War II. Until the end of the 19th Century, it was a tributary state of China. After the Sino-Japanese War (between China and Japan) in 1894 and 1895, Korea experienced a brief and dubious independence, that independence being largely manipulated by Japan. Japan continued pushing the buttons of Korean government to suit its cause for several years, then in 1905 simply dropped all pretext. Korea became a Japanese protectorate for the following 40 years.

World War II ended with the Japanese surrender following President Truman's dramatic nuclear solution. Once the Japanese surrendered, Allied Forces divided Korea in the same manner as Germany and Austria, leaving Soviet and United States forces in trusteeships of portions of the country. Dividing Korea into "North" and "South" along the 38th Parallel, the Soviet Union took trusteeship of the North and the United States of the South.

Naturally, the goal of any of these trusteeships was that, once peace and self-reliance were re-established in the countries, and trustees were certain no undesirable rebellion might be brewing there, the trustees would politely bow out and leave the nations to govern themselves. This goal assumes that the trustees can agree on fundamental ideological matters. Attempts at reunification negotiations failed; concurrently the United States and Soviet Union were recognizing their fundamental differences in new and intimidating ways.

While the United States, in trusteeship of South Korea, pushed for a capitalist government, the Soviet Union in North Korea, with the support of China and the already-established Korean People's Army ("KPA"), quickly formed a socialist government: the Provisional People's Committee for North Korea. The Soviet Union put Kim Il-Sung in charge. In 1948, Soviet forces left North Korea. During 1949, most American forces withdrew from South Korea.

When the Soviet Union and United States stepped away from the dance, so to speak, they left behind on the floor two different countries rather than one, strictly divided in rule and diametrically opposed to one another. Moreover, in both the North and South, the governments wished to claim rule over the entire country of Korea - and as one might expect, there was no desire on either part to compromise when it came to ideology.

In 1947, the United Nations recognized Korea's independence and promoted a democratic election there. In July 1948, Syngman Rhee was overwhelmingly elected as President, thanks to heavy foreign support from the United States, just for example, as Rhee had already met with President Truman to assure him of his own anti-communist philosophies. The Republic of Korea was established in South Korea in August 1948. The Republic of Korea Army ("ROK") was formed. Yet fighting and rioting continued to break out across the South by Northern sympathizers and under Rhee's rule, communists were quickly, often brutally, rounded up, imprisoned, or killed outright.

There had already been rebellion among the Koreans against Japanese rule prior to the conclusion of World War II. The KPA, under the leadership of Kim Il-Sung, led guerilla-style warfare against Japan and then subsequently against South Korea, thus strengthening its ties with China. In fact, when the Chinese civil war saw the victorious People's Republic of China formed in 1949, it was with the physical, troop support of North

Korean forces. The military kinship between China and North Korea was well cemented. Merely a month after the southern half of the Korean peninsula established its democratic government, North Korea declared itself the Democratic People's Republic of Korea, and Kim Il-Sung was made their leader.

The Korean War -
A Chronology of the Chaos

The invasion of South Korea

With World War II only five years past, and continuing upheaval in the Middle East and Asia, and with ever-increasing Cold War concerns, North Korea, through Kim Il-Sung, declared that there could be no united Korea without force. North Korea had both the direct support of the People's Republic of China and the implied support of the Soviet Union, as the Soviet Union had been supplying weapons to North Korea for some time. With the goal of one united, communist-governed Korea in mind, on **June 25, 1950**, the KPA crossed the 38th Parallel to invade South Korea. The KPA, as it advanced, killed off whatever South Korean citizens of import it could locate as well as murdering prisoners of war. They seemed to be an unstoppable force against the unprepared South Korea.

United Nations' Response

Ironically, the protection of South Korea was not of primary concern for the United States or the United Nations. To their thinking, the protection of Europe from the threat of Communism was much more important than the happenings on the Korean peninsula. The United Nations condemned the invasion but was reluctant to authorize involvement, because there was always the risk that the Soviet Union would become directly involved, and with the ready aid of China, spark off another world war. Ultimately the fear of spreading Communism seems to have provoked a greater reaction than the need to protect South Korea itself, particularly after the Soviet Union stated that it was not going to involve itself in the Korean conflict. This, combined with the United States' concerns about the safety of Japan (which seemed to be one of the few, if not the only, key ally that the U.S. had left in that region of the world), finally allowed President Truman to move forward with plans to aid the Republic of Korea.

With the encouragement of President Truman, the United Nations issued Resolution 83 that recommended providing aid to South Korea's government. General Douglas MacArthur, Supreme Commander for the Allied Forces in World War II, was still stationed in Japan and therefore in a perfect position to command movements against North Korea. President Truman ordered MacArthur to aid with air support of evacuations from South Korea as well as to send supplies to the ROK.

Note that in the United States, no formal declaration of war was ever decreed against North Korea. President Truman never asked Congress for a war declaration, but rather asked the United Nations to declare war on North Korea. After all, Korea's current division was a creation of the United Nations in the first place, so it fell to the United Nations to defend it. In the United States, the Korean conflict was not considered a war but a "police action."

Despite having MacArthur and plenty of air support available in Japan, the initial conflict on the ground was a ragged and rushed affair. No major power was prepared for the invasion, and the United States scrambled to send enough troops to merely impede the progress of the KPA - that is, to hold onto what small part of South Korea they could while troops, weapons and tanks were sent as quickly as possible to the site of conflict.

The 24th Infantry Division - Fighting for time

Throughout July and August 1950, this desperate effort was undertaken by a comparative handful of U.S. soldiers. Like MacArthur himself, the 24th Infantry Division was still stationed in occupied Japan and therefore the closest military force the United States had available. The 24th Infantry Division was sent into South Korea via the Pusan Harbor to aid the ROK. Meanwhile, a small band of just more than 500 soldiers, nicknamed Task Force Smith (after their commander) was sent to the hills near Osan to delay the KPA troops in their push south, a heroic effort that nevertheless resulted in dreadful casualties (about one third of the task force) and the capture of a number of soldiers who were subsequently executed by the KPA.

The 24th Infantry Division's assignment, paraphrased, was to simply make conquering South Korea as difficult and time consuming as possible for the KPA, by forcing up figurative roadblocks at every opportunity. The 24th Infantry Division was not equipped to deal with the guns and tanks of the well-stocked KPA, so were repeatedly driven further south while taking the brunt of the aggression and the resulting casualties. They routinely dug themselves into trenches and awaited approaching tanks and troops, held them off for as long as possible and then retreated, again and again. It should also be noted that air support was constantly provided throughout, with bombing sorties flown out of Japan to destroy roads and tanks, and thereby further slow the movement of the KPA.

The KPA invasion, moving ever southward, proved devastating to the 24th Infantry Division, which took more than 10,000 casualties. Eventually the 24th was able to procure a defensible position from the south side of the Nakdong River, establishing a 120-mile perimeter beachhead around the port of Pusan. Roughly ten percent of the entire peninsula was not overrun by the KPA. The U.N. Forces dug in hard to hold Pusan, because if this port city was lost, there would no longer be an access point for U.N. forces and supplies to enter the country. It would mean the end of the war and victory for North Korea.

The 24th Infantry Division, however, performed the assignment it was given, holding out for long enough that the relief and supplies of U.N. Forces could arrive. The methods employed to delay the complete overrun of South Korea finally paid off as gradually the U.N. Forces supplies and troops were bolstered through Pusan. To the advantage of the U.N. Forces, the KPA exhausted its troops and supplies in its ceaseless attempts to overtake the Pusan beachhead.

Help arrives at Pusan

U.N. Forces were not idle throughout the punishing struggle of the 24th Infantry Division and the ROK. Garrisons in Japan sent supplies and troops continuously to Pusan. Perhaps most important was the arrival of much-needed anti-tank artillery and, obviously, much-needed tanks as well. Video taken by an army cameraman in "The Big Picture," a weekly television program detailing military happenings, featured a poignant film clip showing the respect with which the soldiers treated tanks when these behemoth vehicles finally arrived. Tanks were the key to survival for these men, and they were pampered, buffed and polished as if they were classic cars. The tanks were sometimes painted with the faces of tigers, in an attempt to prey on the superstitions of the KPA's soldiers.

With the Pusan beachhead relatively secured and the 24th Infantry Division finally able to recuperate from its long ordeal of delaying the enemy, the U.N. Forces could now focus on repelling the KPA.

United Nations Military Command had determined that KPA supplies were being funneled through Seoul via two major roads from the north. Once supplies reached Seoul they were routed south on a single major road. Therefore retaking Seoul was not only necessary for the morale of South Korea and U.N. Forces, but would serve as a major strike against the KPA. Taking Seoul could most easily be done by invading its port city of Incheon, approximately twenty miles to the west along the Han River, and then moving troops from Incheon to Seoul. Because most of the U.N. forces were fully occupied with holding the ground at the Pusan beachhead, United States troops from northern Japan, the Mediterranean, Hawaii and California were moved to comprise the landing force at Incheon.

Beginning on September 15, 1950, General MacArthur launched an amphibious attack - that is, launching soldiers from ships offshore - on Incheon.

The Incheon landing was complicated by the fact that troop convoys could onto be shipped in at high tide (low tide produced a swampy and unnavigable range around the beach); the first wave of soldiers to hit landfall at high tide were basically on their own for the next ten hours, when the second wave of troops could be moved in on the following high tide.

American military films produced at the time of the Korean War often use the term "softening up" to describe the artillery action employed throughout the war. This is a euphemism that translates to "bombing the hell out of" any area. Battleships at sea and sorties from the air bases blasted the area for hours prior to the Incheon landing. Incheon harbor and surrounding land was "softened up" so thoroughly that the Incheon landing occurred without much fighting or loss of life. The heavy bombardment destroyed most of Incheon and KPA had wisely moved out of the way. In fact, U.N. troops encountered little resistance except in scattered patches on the road to Seoul. U.N. troops reached Seoul by September 26, proceeding without any major resistance except at the last, in the suburbs of Seoul, where KPA troops had dug in hard, sheltered by the many buildings. Clearing them out became a house-by-house affair,

Since the KPA had focused (and exhausted) most of its efforts towards taking the Pusan beachhead, this middle-ground territory of South Korea was not well defended. Now that the UN Forces had a foothold in two sections of Korea: the Pusan beachhead and Incheon, their coverage took a figurative bite out of the overtaken territory of South Korea, flanking the KPA forces on two sides. Many of the KPA troops were unable to withdraw from the territory and were subsequently decimated, resulting in a huge number of casualties and losses for their army.

The retaking of Seoul had the intended consequences of cutting off supply lines to the KPA troops in South Korea, and restoring the government. By September 29, 1950, MacArthur had restored the Republic of Korea and Syngman Rhee as its President.

MacArthur looks north toward China

It is at this point where the plans of President Truman and the plans of General MacArthur began to differ. President Truman instructed MacArthur that the 38th Parallel should not be crossed if there were any signs of Chinese or Soviet forces at work - Truman did not want to antagonize either superpower. But MacArthur did not believe there was room for compromise in the matter of the KPA. He felt that the total surrender of the KPA was the only way to safeguard from Communist expansion, and this would require him to proceed northward toward the Manchurian border.

As October began, KPA forces were steadily driven northward toward the Manchurian border by ROK forces, and within a week U.N. Forces followed, with MacArthur at the head of operations, demanding the surrender of the KPA. U.N. Forces captured Pyongyang, the North Korean capital city, and with the help of massive air support (including vast combat jumps, with hundreds of soldiers parachuting into the battlegrounds), they managed to all but decimate the KPA. The momentum of U.N. Forces looked so promising that MacArthur suggested this was an opportunity to enter China and destroy the supply depots that were serving the KPA. His personal surveys of the battlegrounds indicated no Chinese presence and he reported to President Truman in October 1950 that the Chinese were not a threat to the U.N. forces as they pursued the KPA. Other military intelligence to the president supported this viewpoint, suggesting that while the Chinese might be present in North Korea, there was no evidence that they were planning any action.

China, on the other hand...

China, of course, had been preparing for and even expecting such an outcome since the start of the conflict. They had military intelligence operating in North Korea to keep them abreast of the war's events. Long before U.N. Forces neared China, China's best units were sent to the Manchurian border to form the Northeastern Border Defense Army, the job of which was intervention, if necessary. This army was eventually renamed the People's Volunteer Army (the PVA). China was well-prepared to enter the conflict even as the Soviet Union continued to refuse to directly involve itself.

Chinese troops were ordered into North Korea on October 18, 1950. While MacArthur was assuring Truman that Chinese intervention was a minimal risk, two hundred thousand troops from China were slipping toward the combat zone, utilizing camouflage and night marches to avoid detection by the UN Forces' air support. The PVA soldiers were better trained and far better equipped than their North Korean counterparts, wearing warm uniforms while KPA forces were basically clothed in rags by this time.

By November 26, 1951 the Chinese troops were able to begin launching strong offensives against front-line forces, resulting in losses so heavy that the UN Forces went into retreat, struggling to return south toward the 38th parallel. The PVA's forces managed to split the U.N. Forces in half - the western half scrambling for the 38th parallel, and the eastern half forced into the Chosin reservoir where they had to move, as quickly as possible in the frigid cold, toward the harbor city of Hungnam to be evacuated before the PVA could catch up with them.

In mid-December, China took over leadership of the KPA in addition to its own PVA, removing Kim Il-Sung from command of the forces. For the remainder of the hostilities in the Korean War, China made the decisions concerning North Korea's protection, invasions and negotiations.

Evacuation at Hungnam

Forced to flee from the KPA, to the port of Hungnam on the eastern seaboard of the Korean peninsula, U.N. Forces conducted a remarkable evacuation by sea, basically using its "invasion by sea" protocol in reverse, loading landing craft on the beach and returning repeatedly to the battleships and carriers waiting on the Japan Sea. The evacuation was on a massive scale, including not only U.N. troops, but all of their equipment. They wanted nothing left behind for North Korean forces to use. Extraneous materials were burned on the spot.

Not only were the U.N. Forces setting out from Hungnam as quickly as possible, but thousands of North Korean refugees came as well, desperate to go south with them, fearing the return of North Korean rule and seeking out livable terrain after their homeland had been devastated by bombardment attacks. The staggering evacuation statistics include the removal of just more than 100,000 soldiers, almost 100,000 civilians, more than 17,000 vehicles and 3.5 tons of supplies to Pusan.

The last U.N. troops to leave Hungnam destroyed the harbor as they went, a line of TNT packed along the harbor and detonated from sea, sending the entire harbor crashing into the ocean, useless to enemy forces.

General Ridgway's operations

The Chinese attack had swiftly driven U.N. Forces out of North Korea, and the city of Seoul once more fell to the enemy; this was the second time the city was lost. Having performed a highly successful invasion thus far, Chinese forces paused in the advance to recuperate their troops, under the false assumption that U.N. Forces in the south would be too demoralized to strike back. This was a miscalculation, for in reality the fall of Seoul to Communist troops a second time actually served to motivate troops in the South and invigorate them to push back against the Communist invasion. General Matthew Ridgway was aware of this tendency in the PVA forces: after a hard push, they would cease most activity and regroup and refit for a week or so.

General Ridgway intended to take advantage of this. He capably took charge of the response, and far sooner than the enemy had expected, retaliated to push the PVA back above the 38th Parallel. By late January 1951, General Ridgway had regrouped troops to begin **Operation**

Thunderbolt to halt further progression into the south by the PVA, and to hold the territory south of the Han River (which is directly south of Seoul).

U.N. forces, given a chance to regroup and resupply in South Korea, were then rallied by General Ridgway to begin **Operation Killer**, (from February 20, 1951 through March 6, 1951) the point of which is obvious enough in its name; it was a complex plan of several divisions taking various roads and course-ways northward to destroy as many Chinese troops as was possible. U.N. Forces proceeded slowly northward, killing or capturing what Chinese troops they could, but the resistance to their attack was not as heavy as expected, and after an initially bloody series of attacks, the KPA and PVA forces seemed to be in full retreat.

U.N. Forces fought all the way back to Seoul and retook the city yet again in the subsequent **Operation Ripper**, more easily this time as the Chinese troops had largely abandoned the area. It seemed that Chinese troops were not willing to take a strong defensive stance below the 38th parallel and had begun an early withdrawal to the north.

MacArthur is removed from command

General MacArthur's actions came under scrutiny chiefly because of his behavior concerning China. MacArthur had already shown a misunderstanding of China's willingness to enter the conflict, prior to their crushing entry into North Korea. After the Chinese PVA had entered the war full scale, MacArthur continued to bait and antagonize them with threats of nuclear weapons (not authorized by President Truman) and demands for complete surrender (again, against Truman's intentions and orders).

Mixed messages were in play, as General MacArthur also received permissions contradictory to the president's. While the president wanted no entry above the 38th Parallel unless Chinese interference was obvious, MacArthur had received word from the United States' Defense Secretary George Marshall, stating that MacArthur should feel "unhampered tactically and strategically to proceed north of the 38th parallel." (A point of interest: Secretary Marshall was later subjected to intense scrutiny by Joseph McCarthy as a communist sympathizer.) Continuing this trend toward vague instructions, the Joint Chiefs of Staff had also sent MacArthur directives that he was to destroy the KPA and unify the country of Korea under President Rhee, but once again, not if the Chinese or Soviets seemed prepared they were going to intervene. These ambiguous and open-ended instructions would come back to haunt President Truman when MacArthur chose to act in pursuit of his goal for complete victory (going so far as to antagonize the Chinese government directly and assure foreign leaders that he wanted to go to war against China) and nobody on President Truman's side was able to say that MacArthur specifically disobeyed orders, leaving the decision on whether or not MacArthur should be removed from command almost entirely in Truman's hands.

After the strong victory of General Ridgway in turning back the Chinese invasion, and with the return of the North and South Korean forces to their respective sides of the 38th Parallel by March 1951, President Truman wanted to use this time as an opportunity for negotiations to stop the war.

General MacArthur, however, was adamant in the belief that victory must be total - he insisted that if Communism was permitted to win in North Korea, it would create a domino effect of communist takeovers that would extend throughout Asia and Europe. MacArthur was, by all indications, willing or even eager to take the war to China (and thus the Soviet Union). The United Nations grew increasingly worried about

MacArthur's pushes toward China, for McArthur believed that the only option for this war was complete victory. China and the Soviet Union, however, had formed a pact stating that either country would come to the aid of the other if they were attacked, and MacArthur's continued aggressions toward China could believably lead to World War III.

Secret intercepts of communications between General MacArthur and foreign ambassadors in Tokyo suggested that MacArthur wanted to use the Korean War as a precursor to war with China. This knowledge enraged President Truman but he was unable to use them as evidence against the general, precisely because they were "secret" intercepts.

A controversy that never reached resolution is General MacArthur's willingness, or lack thereof, to use nuclear weapons in the Korean conflict. In December 1950, MacArthur put in a request to have discretion to employ nuclear weapons, but only as a fallback. He created and submitted a list of targets in China and Korea which would require 34 bombs. By this time in the war, a certain number of nuclear weapons had been tentatively designated for use against the Chinese or Soviets "just in case" (as is always the reason for weapons stockpiling in a Cold War), because the Joint Chiefs were concerned about the increasing number of Soviet forces in the Far East, and they authorized MacArthur to use them in response to an attack. But President Truman, among others, was highly concerned about MacArthur's using the weapons ahead of schedule or necessity. This was not precisely because MacArthur had threatened to do so, but because of his attitude toward the need for total victory over communism. The question of whether MacArthur was for or against nuclear weapons remains unanswered. But having nuclear weapons in the hands of a commander determined to win - particularly when that commander repeatedly pushes the limits of his instructions or takes the course of the war onto himself -

was enough to cause serious concerns about MacArthur's continued leadership.

President Truman was forced to take the action more or less on his own, without the solid support of his Joint Chiefs and advisors - or in a word, most were willing to admit that General MacArthur was "pushing it," that he was "stretching" his duties and crossing the line in many cases but that they couldn't really say he had directly disobeyed any orders.

Serendipity seemed to be at work on President Truman's side, however, as General MacArthur wrote a letter to Truman criticizing the president's policy and warning that failure to eliminate the Communist threat in Asia would lead to the fall of Europe to communism. The letter was read aloud to the House of Representatives by one of Truman's opponents, a fact that would allow Truman to accuse MacArthur of insubordination or, at least, a failure to follow presidential orders. On April 10, 1951, Truman ordered MacArthur's removal from command and replaced him with General Ridgway.

That the enormously popular General Douglas MacArthur was relieved of his command was an enormously unpopular decision made by President Truman. MacArthur was a national hero from WWII, and outspoken in his desire to basically obliterate communism or its possible spread across Europe - a sentiment that was echoed in the minds of the general American public living in fear of the dreaded Red Menace. MacArthur returned to the United States to a hero's welcome, including a ticker-tape parade in his honor. He gave a retirement speech before Congress that immortalized the words "old soldiers never die; they just fade away," and was interrupted by fifty ovations as he spoke. He was personally visited by Japanese Emperor Hirohito and his name even bandied around as a possible presidential candidate.

Truman's decision to fire the general was followed by increasing troubles in his presidency and extremely low approval ratings. It should be noted, however, that by June 1951, congressional hearings determined that MacArthur had violated the Constitution by defying presidential orders, and that President Truman had been within his powers to relieve MacArthur of command. Though it suffered at the end of his term and he chose not to seek re-election, historically speaking, President Truman's reputation as a leader has since been restored and his decisions are seen as correct and necessary courses of action.

Stalemate, or, we've crossed the peninsula....again

In June 1951, the KPA and PVA were north of the 38th Parallel, and the ROK and U.N. Forces had retaken their territory in the south. With the exception of the presence of China's PVA, the situation was more or less the same as it had been prior to the onset of the war.

At this point, you have probably noticed that the Korean War seemed to play out like a see-saw, with the Korean peninsula being crossed four times by three different armies:

1. The KPA crossed the 38th Parallel, invaded South Korea and pushed forces down to the southern beachhead of Pusan;

2. U.N. Forces drove the KPA back northward, crossed the 38th Parallel and pushed northward toward the Yalu River and Manchurian border.

3. The PVA crossed the Manchurian border and drove U.N. Forces either south or to the port city of Hungnam, forcing U.N.'s evacuation of the north.

4. U.N. Forces under the command of General Ridgway and the succession of Operation Thunderbolt, Operation Killer and Operation Ripper, forced the PVA back north above the 38th Parallel.

The Korean War devolved into a lengthy and costly series of battles, advances and retreats in waves as territory was taken, retaken and then retaken again. The power of both sides was based on the willingness of superpowers to go only so far in their aggression, no one willing to take a step to start a third World War and, at the same time, neither side willing to concede on the issue that started the conflict: the democratic status of a united Korea.

From this point forward in the war, territorial skirmishes did little but move the battling army's lines in negligible distances north or southward. The battlefront became the series of "Hill Battles," which involved warring over vantage points along the ever-changing border, with famous names: Heartbreak Ridge, Bunker Hill, Sniper Ridge, Bloody Ridge, T-Bone, the Hook, the Punchbowl, Luke's Castle, and Old Baldy. The Korean War turned into a trench war similar to World War I, with two sides dug in opposite one another with a no-man's-land between them, and the ongoing fighting was for mere patches of ground.

The Korean War continued in this manner until June 1953, close to two years of ongoing yet unproductive conflict. This type of warfare was bad for troop morale as well as public support, for without the dazzle of large-scale battles and operations, the futility of the conflict became increasingly obvious. U.N. Forces began to question their presence, with soldiers far from home wondering exactly what they were fighting for. Public interest in the war waned. The desire for resolution intensified as time passed yet no resolution could be agreed upon.

27

Armistice: How the War Finally Stopped, Without Actually Ending

Peace talks begin poorly in Kaesong

Cease-fire talks began in June 1951 in the town of Kaesong and were attended by General Ridgway and his staff, but it was clear from the beginning that the North Korean generals in attendance were not authorized to actually make decisions on behalf of their army. They were proxies, reporting back to superiors (i.e., China and the PVA) for instructions.

Moreover, the Communist propaganda machine made numerous attempts to "spin" the talks not as a negotiation, but as a United Nations surrender, carefully staging photographs of U.N. military being searched by North Korean soldiers, allowing armed North Korean troops inside the negotiations area (which was against the agreed-upon terms), and heavily censoring information that was released about the said negotiations. Neither side trusted the other to truthfully report the events that were taking place; American film reel of the time is guilty of insulting and minimizing Communist officers and needless name-calling (i.e., double-talking Communists).

At one point, an angered General Ridgway, who could easily see the way that he and his staff were being played, insisted that United Nations reporters be allowed to attend the talks. This was permitted, but later that same day, the United Nations reporters were stopped by armed Communist forces on the return journey to their camp. Under intimidation they were told that they were not permitted to report on any of the happenings inside the negotiations. The reporters returned at once to General Ridgway to inform him of the implied threats and censorship.

General Ridgway demanded respectful treatment as an ultimatum if the talks were to continue, which, at least temporarily, let the talks resume without further excessive Communist-propaganda interference. It seemed hardly worth the trouble that General Ridgway took, however. The cease-fire talks that continued from June through August were preoccupied with preamble, engaging in excessive negotiations to prepare for negotiations. Where should the peace talks be held and what should their agenda be? A formal agenda of talking points was not even agreed upon on until August. While the squabbling over the logistics of the meeting itself went on, the North Korean forces were able to restock and reinforce their troops on the battleground, and the trench war between the two sides continued to pass territory back and forth uselessly while lives were lost and land was destroyed.

Talks proceeded slowly, when they proceeded at all. Long intervals fell between meetings, sometimes weeks at a time while investigations took place of perceived injustices. Kaesong as a location was eventually contaminated by the insistence of North Korea that the site had been bombed. No proof of the bombing was ever discovered, but the Communists refused to continue negotiations there and talks were moved to Panmunjom, a village close to both North and South Korea, with the stipulation that both powers protect the village.

Peace talks resume at a snail's pace

Peace talks were driven largely by China and the United Nations. Neither North Korean nor South Korean governments wished to cease fighting until the country was unified. It was only under pressure from their superpower supporters that either side agreed to attempt negotiations, and President Rhee continued to oppose them in spite of his congress's agreement to allow negotiations on South Korea's behalf.

Peace talks resumed at Panmunjom, a village about ten miles to the east of Kaesong, and dragged on for almost two years (1951-1953). The talks were again bogged down by patently ridiculous delays including almost prank-like behaviors (the KPA/PVA sawed down the chair legs of the U.N. representatives so that the representatives would appear shorter than their communist opponents) or one-upmanship about the size of the countries' flags at the meeting. The participants were so preoccupied with appearances and saving face that such trivial matters could put a stop to negotiations for weeks at a time.

Brigadier General S.L.A. Marshall, whom we have previously mentioned as a prominent, but rather biased, military analyst, claimed on "The Big Picture" that the behavior of the Communist parties at the negotiations in both Kaesong and Panmunjom was predictable. In Mao Tse-Tung's Communist Manifesto of 1945, the Chinese leader stated that the negotiation table is a battlefield, and tactics to "delay and demoralize" the enemy should be taken there. Therefore, it should be no surprise that the Communist participants, including the KPA which answered to China, took such pains to make the negotiations untenable. To what lengths the U.N. Forces responded in kind is unknown; General Marshall did not comment on that.

A truly time-worthy, major point of contention that stalled agreement for months was the point of POW (prisoner of war) repatriation. 150,000 PVA and KPA prisoners of war were held by the United Nations Forces, and 10,000 by the communists, and some method had to be decided as to what would happen to these people after the war. Repatriation means simply the return of prisoners to their homelands and ostensibly to freedom. The sticking point? Many of the PVA and KPA refused repatriation, having no desire to return to North Korea or China, a fact that those countries found unacceptable (to a lesser extent, some United Nations and South Korean prisoners of war did not wish to leave North Korea).

Eisenhower goes to Korea

During the 1952 presidential campaign, Dwight D. Eisenhower took a hard line against government corruption, communism, and Korea - all three things that he could accuse the Truman Administration of failing to fix. This was in spite of the fact that he and President Truman had formerly been friends. Eisenhower took advantage of the widespread fear of the Red Menace by raising the question of Latin America and the unchecked communism spreading there. His campaign criticized the Democratic Party for allowing Soviet spies to infiltrate the government. The Democrats were also accused of failing to properly prepare for war, resulting in the hectic start of, and we might also guess by extension, the failure to win, the Korean War. In a campaign speech close to election time, Eisenhower told his audience that he would visit Korea personally to see about ending the war; keep in mind, however, that he claimed liberation of communist countries should be conducted by peaceful means. As a highly respected general and a World War II hero, this was precisely what the American public wanted to hear, and it was the boost he needed to take the election.

As had been his political promise, President-elect Eisenhower went to view first-hand the ongoing conflict in Korea in the later months of 1952, shortly after his Presidential victory. Here of course he could see the results of the ongoing stalemate and its costs both literally and figuratively. Eisenhower's policies, at least in theory, brooked no discord from China, for he threatened to use nuclear force if an armistice was not reached. This sounds like a rather different tact than his "peaceful means only" campaign speeches. Is it possible that Eisenhower was bluffing, or was he indeed willing to launch a nuclear war? Luckily no one had to find out the answer to that question.

In 1953, the death of Joseph Stalin caused the Soviet Union to withdraw some of its support for China, and without that superpower backing it, China finally agreed to compromise on the issue of war prisoners. In the end, a combination of the United States' warnings and the sudden diversion of the Soviet Union's attention appear to have been the motivation China needed to ease up on its demands.

An armistice was finally signed on July 27, 1953, and it, as well as the borders put into effect, remain unchanged to this day, although recent events lead one to believe that North and South Korea are willing to try mending their differences insofar as their own peninsula is concerned. Eisenhower's biographer, Stephen Ambrose, attributes the Korean armistice as a great achievement in the president's administration and eloquently expresses Eisenhower's realization that the war of attrition in Korea was unwinnable, while resorting to out-and-out nuclear war was "unthinkable."

The terms of the Armistice

The Korean Armistice Agreement was signed by representatives of the United Nations Command, the Korean People's Army and the Chinese

People's Volunteer Army. President Syngman Rhee of the Republic of Korea refused to sign, as he did not accept the failure to unite Korea.

The Armistice's major components were:

1.   The establishment of the Korean Demilitarized Zone
2.   A cease-fire
3.   Repatriation of prisoners of war.

The impasse regarding the status of repatriation had proved so insurmountable that eventually the question had to be handed off to a neutral committee. This was the Neutral Nations Repatriation Commission that was led by India. In the final decision made by the Committee, each side was compelled to return all prisoners of war who *insisted* on repatriation (i.e., those who did not want to return would not be forced to do so). Ultimately more than 22,000 KPA and PVA soldiers refused to be returned to their countries, and close to 400 United Nations soldiers refused repatriation.

The Cease Fire was monitored by the "Armistice Commission," which included five United Nations officials and five Communist officials. The Armistice Commission dealt with disputes that arose regarding the terms of Armistice. The feeling of the United Nations at the time was that it must convey an image of strength in these negotiations, otherwise the Communist members might perceive an opportunity to take advantage and gain ground - it isn't hard to imagine that the Communist members assume the same, and behave in much the same way.

Ironically, the international border is not vastly different from that established by the 38th Parallel demarcation.

What exactly is the Demilitarized Zone?

A provision of the Korean Armistice created a demilitarized zone (the "DMZ") that would act as a type of neutral zone between North and South Korea. It stretches laterally from one side of the peninsula to the other, more or less dividing the peninsula in half, and is about 2.5 miles wide. Inside the DMZ is a secured area where negotiations can occur, referred to as the Joint Security Area, but otherwise no one is allowed in the area except for military personnel. Civilians who happened to live inside the area were forced to leave.

As an example of the strictness of the zone's boundaries, a Korean landmark of historical significance was rendered inaccessible because it happened to fall inside the DMZ. The monk/ruler Gun Ye's legacy led to the Goryeo dynasty (918-1392), which reigned over the united country of Korea; "Goryeo" is in fact the origin of the name "Korea." With the Armistice put into effect, the Castle of Gun Ye, Gun Ye's tomb and the ruins of his capital city, Taebong, all lie within the DMZ and are inaccessible to Koreans for either tourism or study.

Out of a combination of caution and suspicion, an additional zone of land buffers the DMZ. This is the Civilian Control Zone (or sometimes called the Civilian Control Line), which ranges in width from about three to twelve miles. The Civilian Control Zone serves as a deterrent and a safety net of sorts, to prevent civilians from interfering with activities in the DMZ (and, in turn, to keep those civilians safe). The Civilian Control Zone was actually devised by the U.S. Army and it became effective about a year after the DMZ was established. The military, serving as both monitor and protector to those who live there or otherwise enter, guards the Civil Control Zone. The Line is blocked with barbed wire fencing and patrolled. These intimidating details make the Civilian Control Line the public face of the DMZ, as photographing the actual DMZ is illegal. Over the years since the Armistice, several infiltration tunnels have been discovered burrowed beneath the DMZ.

35

The Korean War,
Up Close and Personal

Now that we have covered the chronology of the war, and unofficial conclusion, let us look to the more personal aspects of the fighting. Wars are conducted from the high towers, but they are fought and often won by the infantry on the ground. Technology invariably booms in wartime, with inventions and innovations meant to either take more lives, or save more lives in return. The Korean War was different from previous conflicts in a number of ways (its landscape a primary example); some out-of-the-box thinking was required in order for forces to adapt.

The savage and savaged terrain of Korea

In the back-and-forth fighting, the land of Korea itself was savaged and the infrastructure was repeatedly destroyed. Armies basically had to build roads and bridges as they went, because in retreat, all such things would be destroyed to keep the enemy armies from using them. We have already discussed the number of passes made over the land, and each advance of one army meant the retreat of another. Therefore, infrastructure and roads were repeatedly built and destroyed. Soldiers on the march could expect at any moment to have to clear a road, build a bridge, cross a river or climb a mountain.

Soldiers fighting in Korea were subject to some of the most merciless conditions encountered in modern warfare. Korea experiences the gamut of difficult weather: bitter cold temperatures in winter, a violent rainy season that leaves the terrain an ocean of mud, and sweltering heat and humidity in summer months. Korean War Pilot Chuck Frost, speaking to WCCC-TV in Waco, recalled that often the U.S. troops would bomb a bridge to stop the Korean supply lines, only to see the trucks then able to cross the rivers anywhere, merely by driving across the thick ice. The Japan Sea can generate typhoons powerful enough to tear apart buildings. Ships on the Japan Sea were forced to endure violent winter storms and huge, roiling waves, typical of the region and season. Planes on aircraft carriers had to take off and land on icy decks in temperatures that reached as low as five degrees below zero in the month of December.

Special uniforms were developed by the United States military in order to keep its soldiers from hypothermia and frostbite, from heavy parkas to winter boots large enough to accommodate the three pairs of socks issued in order to protect feet and toes. In Army footage from the time, one can often see American soldiers bundled in parkas and heavy clothes until only their eyes show from beneath their hoods, as they ride side by side on rolling tanks. Heavy mittens were designed with trigger-fingers sewn in, so that soldiers could use their guns without removing the mittens, which they then often did on the frozen ground of the Korean mountains. The frightening retreat to Hungnam, and the improvised evacuation thereafter, occurred during the coldest months of the year.

Almost as difficult as the violent winter was the rainy season that followed, which left any remaining roads (those not destroyed by bombing raids) ruined. Rivers swelled violently. The troops who crossed Korean countryside back and forth during the northward-southward and near constant movement of the armies were forced to simply build bridges and roads as they were needed, often using Korean civilians to help with the process. As the war of attrition would dictate, regions were overtaken and abandoned, overtaken and abandoned, repeatedly, and when one army left an area they destroyed roads and bridges, which only meant the next occupying force was required to rebuild everything. The United States military quickly developed a number of vehicles capable of submersion, including waterproofed tanks, jeeps and transport trucks. The excessive rain and mud meant that air-dropping supplies was essential, and whereas in previous conflicts, air-dropping supplies was considered an emergency measure, in Korea it became standard practice out of necessity.

Troop integration

Segregation is never right, but on a battlefield of soldiers all fighting for the same cause, it seems particularly ludicrous. The Civil Rights Movement was on the horizon, and the Korean War saw the first integration of United States military units. President Truman had issued an executive order in 1948 that called for the equal treatment of black soldiers. The beginning of the Korean conflict still saw a few instances of unit segregation, as military branches differed in the speed at which the executive order was put into action. Nevertheless, in October 1951 the last segregated unit was deactivated.

I think I recognize that soldier...

Looking back on a war, one can always find soldiers who went on to have famous careers. The Korean conflict was no different. Of course, all soldiers are superstars, but, just for fun, here is a list of celebrities who proved themselves in the Korean conflict.

> » Both the first and second man to walk on the moon, future Apollo 11 astronauts **Neil Armstong** and **Buzz Aldrin** were Air Force pilots during the conflict, and flew 78 missions and 68 missions respectively.

» **John Glenn**, a veteran of both World War II and Korea, was a Marine fighter pilot and became the first American man to orbit Earth as one of the famous Mercury Astronauts.

» Singer **Johnny Cash** monitored Soviet radio transmissions in his role with the Air Force. He wrote many of his early songs while in the service.

» Actor **James Garner** was decorated with two Purple Hearts for injuries he sustained while he served in the 5th Regimental Combat Team.

» Actor **Michael Caine** was a member of the British Army's 1st Battalion Royal Fusiliers and saw heavy fighting.

» Celebrity personality/sidekick **Ed McMahon** was a highly decorated Marine pilot who flew up to five missions a day. McMahon was also a flight instructor in World War II.

» DJ and voice actor **Casey Kasem** was an on-air personality in the Armed Forces Radio Korea Network.

» Hall-of-Fame baseball stars **Ted Williams** and **Whitey Ford** both served. Williams was a World War II veteran who was drafted into service in Korea after only six games of the 1952 baseball season. He flew 39 missions for the Marines (often with John Glenn!) and won three medals during his service. As Williams was a record-setting baseball star, fans of the game can only imagine what his statistics could have been, if he'd been on the baseball field for those three seasons. Ford, who went on to be part of the "Big Four" of the Yankees' 1953 powerhouse pitching staff, was in the Army in Korea during 1951 and 1952. Of our listed celebrities, baseball players Ted Williams and Whitey Ford seem to be the only ones who were already famous when the conflict began.

» No United States president actively served in the Korean War. **President Jimmy Carter** was in the Navy at the time of the Korean War but was stationed stateside.

Medical innovation: Organization, and a helicopter

Medical innovation greatly reduced the number of deaths among wounded U.N. Troops. Overall the treatment of casualties was streamlined, resulting in a lower mortality rate among United Nations soldiers than in previous conflicts, including World War II.

From the point of the battlefield, casualties were routed through an organized, triaged system that helped ensure those with the most serious injuries were treated first, and quickly. Their first stop was a battalion aid station, where life-saving measures could take place followed by quick evacuation. Evacuation was performed by Jeep, or ambulance if the roads were passable. This in itself was an entirely different problem: Korean roads were in poor shape, frequently flooded, and targeted to such an extent that Jeep transport was often impossible, and ambulances were frequently a target of enemy fire and were required to cover their medical logos.

The difficulty transporting wounded over the various troublesome terrains of Korea forced a rethinking of the system. The helicopter, which had been used only briefly in World War II, now became a major part of many military operations, not the least of which was the transportation of wounded. For the first time on a large scale, air evacuation of casualties was possible, thanks to the inclusion of the modified helicopter. Helicopters were specially fitted with stretchers, one on each side of the cockpit, in which wounded patients could be securely carried in covered, heated capsules until they arrived at the next care station. The use of the Medevac helicopter carried on after the war and is now a common life-saving practice.

The Regimental Collecting Stations included mobile hospitals (the M*A*S*H units with which many of us know from television) and Division Clearing Stations. These facilities were basic and strictly purposed to save lives, without any extraneous luxuries or amenities. From this point, patients still in need of care could be evacuated, again by air, to hospitals in Japan, and thereafter, more than half were returned to the United States to complete their treatment.

In a related but unexpected way, helicopters also saved lives and prevented casualties on the battlefield. Here helicopters were used for the first time in combat as a method to deliver soldiers to a battleground "fresh," meaning the poor guys didn't have to march five miles through weather extremes and destroyed landscapes to reach the site of the fighting. Helicopters could drop the troops off on a hilltop, the troops could set up operations or perform their mission, and then be airlifted right back out if they were no longer needed. They could take the high ground in a fight, without ever having to fight their way to it.

Naval support during the war

Clearly the U.N. Forces were supported constantly by aircraft during the conflict. Bombers, jets and helicopters have been shown throughout this overview to have played a major role. But of course naval support was also crucial to troop support, and in the case of fighter jets, made that aspect of aerial support possible in the first place. After all, where is a fighter jet going to land, if not on an aircraft carrier? Aircraft carriers were among the battleships, providing landing and takeoff zones for the jet air fighters that were used for the first time in the Korean War. These smaller aircraft could not be flown in from Japan as were the bombers, therefore the constant maintenance of the carriers was of critical importance.

Throughout the conflict, U.N. Forces were aided by non-stop naval support. Battleships were stationed off the coast of Korea in strategic locations to provide a near-constant artillery barrage of targets. Missiles from battleships could be directed at targets as far as twenty kilometers away. Artillery flung at the enemy was also useful in "scouting" the terrain prior to aquatic landings, letting troops know ahead of time where the enemies were hiding. This tactic was crucial in the taking of Incheon and subsequently Seoul (the first time), because the "softening" of the enemy before the landing of the troops left U.N. Forces with almost no opposition in the march on Seoul. Battleships also conducted minesweeping and aided in resupply operations. And of course, the evacuation of Hungnam could never have been accomplished without the quick response of the naval forces.

War crimes: the expected and the unexpected

Neither side of this conflict can be found innocent of committing crimes against innocents; the number of civilian casualties alone (estimated at over two million of the total four million casualties of the war) attests to this. Both North and South Korean governments executed thousands of suspected traitors to their respective cause, but of course these types of political execution had been going on long before the war broke out.

Politically motivated massacres occurred on both sides of the 38th Parallel, perpetrated by the ROK and the KPA; in the instance of the ROK, President Syngman Rhee frequently ordered the deaths of communist sympathizers, as well as their families. In fact, investigations conducted in recent years have suggested that South Korea was responsible for roughly eighty percent of civilian massacres, whereas North Korea is believed to be responsible for only eighteen percent. South Korea's own army suffered the consequences of corruption; some of its soldiers starved to death on their marches because of the embezzlement of their food supplies. As for military casualties, on the battlefield, prisoners of war were sometimes simply executed on the spot rather than their captors going through the difficulty of moving the prisoners, while the territories of the war changed rapidly back and forth. Unfortunately, American soldiers shot several hundred civilians outright as often refugees were suspected of being disguised KPA soldiers.

Prisoners of war on both sides endured ideological lecturing, missionary work, or outright brainwashing, and were subjected to maiming and torture. Chinese POWs who underwent this experience were typically arrested and forced through reprogramming upon their return to China. U.N. POWs fared no better, being beaten and starved, subjugated to brainwashing, and even sometimes marched to death.

Prisoners of war from the United States were not prepared to withstand the intense levels of communist indoctrination forced upon them while they were captured. The KPA and PVA were willing to use extreme violence and mental torture to force prisoners into statements or behaviors that favored the communist agenda; a deadly side effect of this treatment was to decrease the moral support and chain of command among the prisoners.

This unexpected phenomenon led to the creation of the Code of the United States Fighting Force, which included the implementation of training for troops on how to withstand indoctrination to the best of their abilities.

The Code of Conduct: What does it mean? Does it work?

The written Military Code of Conduct contains six articles of guidance regarding behavior on the battlefield and after capture, including the well-known adage of giving only "name, rank and serial number." The Code's Articles specifically reference situations that no doubt arose in North Korean POW camps: troops were never to surrender themselves or the members of their command voluntarily, they were to make all efforts toward resistance and escape for themselves and other prisoners; they were to maintain the chain of command even in a prison situation and "keep faith" with fellow prisoners; they were not to accept any special favors from the enemy; and they were not to make disloyal statements to their country.

We might wonder how much use such a code would actually be to an imprisoned soldier, under the duress of fear and torture. Al Erickson, chief of operational support at Joint Services Survival, Evasion, Resistance and Escape Agency, confirms the Code's usefulness in providing a sense of purpose and dignity to captured soldiers by giving them a moral guide. In an article regarding the Code's effectiveness by Major Donna Miles, Erickson is quoted as saying that former U.S. POWs have called it "a lifesaver that gave them something to hold onto during their captivity."

After the Korean War

Financial cost of the war

The United States spent an estimated $15 billion dollars (that's 1950s' billions, remember) on the Korean War. This set a precedent of high defense budget spending that has continued through the decades.

Rebuilding South Korea

In the years following the Armistice, U.S. military personnel remained behind in South Korea to assist in the rebuilding of the devastated country. In the immediate aftermath of the war, American soldiers helped establish makeshift orphanages for the heartbreaking numbers of Korean children fending for themselves in the ruins. Several hundred thousand dollars were donated personally by American troops to help children and towns rise from the rubble. The Armed Forces Assistance to Korea (AFAK) project built offices, libraries, schools and factories for both light and heavy industry. Army specialists aided in the construction of communication lines, roads and bridges. Frequently Korean civilians were used to help in the construction, using materials scavenged from the innumerable bombed-out sites. The South Korean railroad was reconstructed. Flood control measures were put in place, as the rainy season could result in dangerous flooding (the landscape being far too damaged for natural flood control to work). The ROK Army ranks were refilled and trained by the U.S. Military, and the two groups worked side by side in the rehabilitation of villages and the patrolling of the DMZ.

The modern DMZ

One amazing result of the DMZ was the inadvertent creation of a virtually untouched natural preserve. Because no human activity has been allowed on the land in well over sixty years, and because of the fortuitous number of varied environments that cross the country (from mountains to swamps) the activity of nature has overtaken the zone, allowing it to become home to several endangered species of plants and animals. Surveys of the region are now permitted, which have produced astonishing results: 2,900 plant species; 70 types of mammals; and 320 bird species. Efforts to turn the area into a National Park or a biosphere area for widespread study are being debated; North Korea has disagreed for the most part saying that the creation of a biosphere breaks the rules of the Armistice.

North Korea after Armistice

North Korea maintained its alliances with China and the Soviet Union despite the tensions between those two superpowers. The last of the Chinese troops left in October 1958 and it was at this time that North Korea was fully realized as an independent nation.

North Korea suffered the highest damages in the war, both to its physical land and to its civilian population. Even so, within ten years its production levels had matched those of 1949 and its economy continued to thrive until the Soviet Union's dissolution, which put an end to Soviet aid to the country. Leader Kim Il-Sung remained in power until his death in 1994. He was succeeded by his son Kim Jong-il, then his grandson Kim Jong-un. The family line has established a "cult of personality" around their bloodline, which, in simplified terms, enforces the belief that the well-being of the nation itself relies on their family's leadership.

Today North Korea describes itself as a self-reliant socialist state with a "military first" philosophy. The country presently has the fourth-largest army in the world.

South Korea after Armistice

Modern South Korea rose from the ashes of the Korean War with considerable struggle. It has undergone numerous changes in leadership and policy since the time of the war and for about forty years following the Armistice it was controlled by a series of autocratic rulers separated in time by brief periods of political ambiguity. Considering its location, the pressures of its neighboring countries and the diversity of ideology within its own population, this is not surprising.

Syngman Rhee remained president of South Korea until the April 19 Revolution (1960) when the level of the corruption in his rule was exposed to the public. This led to his resignation. Leaderless, the country was rudderless for over a year until General Park Chung-hee took the position by coup. Under Park, the South Korean economy and infrastructure boomed, but his policies of political repression and technically limitless term of power defined him as more of a military dictator than a democratic leader. He ruled for 17 years until his assassination.

A second coup and takeover occurred leaving General Chun Doo-hwan in charge. He placed the nation under strict military rule from 1979 until 1987. The corruption of his government was exposed, leading to the June Democracy Movement - where, again, nationwide protests led to change. At that time, the Democratic Justice Party was able to promote the direct election of Roh-Tae-Wood. The Sixth Republic rose out of the political conflict and remains in place today.

South Korea became recognized as a democracy in 1997 with the election of Kim Dae-jung, who has been able to lead the nation in the gradual recovery of the economy that was lost under Chun Doo-hwan's military rule and the subsequent turmoil.

Today, South Korea is a highly developed, innovative and technologically forward country with an impressive economy (the 12th largest in the world) and a booming pop-culture scene.

Status of South and North Korea in the United Nations

Here are some quick statistics concerning the relationship between the United Nations and the Korean peninsula countries:

South Korea has had observer status at the U.N. since 1948, and North Korea since 1971.

South Korea has had a non-permanent seat on the U.N. Security Counsel twice, but North Korea never has.

The United Nations admitted both the Republic of Korea (South Korea) and the Democratic People's Republic of Korea (North Korea) in 1991.

Han Seung-soo of South Korea was president of the United Nations General Assembly in 2001; in 2006 and 2011, South Korean Ban Ki-moon was elected as Secretary General.

The United Nations annually condemns the human rights violations of North Korea, a country that has one of the world's most terrible reputations for such crimes. The list of violations is grave indeed, including, but not limited to, restrictions on freedom of speech and the incarceration of political prisoners, torture and "re-education" of prisoners, forced labor camps, arbitrary detention, child labor, religious persecution, strict travel restrictions inside and outside the country, abductions, forced prostitution, forced abortions, and even restrictions to food access. The United Nations voted in favor of referring North Korea to the International Criminal Court in 2014, for human rights violations.

North Korea denies the allegations and responds that these accusations are politically motivated. It holds that human rights are conditional, not universal, and that the rights of the collective take precedent over the rights of individuals. North Korea's government guarantees the rights of its people, it claims, but will not guarantee those same rights to anyone who opposes socialism or the interests of the government itself, which sounds like a set of criteria very open to interpretation.

China's Outcome

Protection of the Manchurian Border was vital to China, as the region contained the country's most important industrial centers. In that regard, its campaign can be considered successful. In preserving the country of North Korea, China also managed to secure a significant geographical distance between itself and an ally of the United States.

In the process of protecting its North Korean ally, though, China missed an opportunity to retake the Republic of China (Taiwan), as the United States was obligated to protect the small country due to its commitment against the Cold War. For this context, we provide an extremely simplified version of events, because Taiwan, much like Korea, has a complex history of rule by other countries including both China and Japan. Detailing the politics and tensions involved between China and Taiwan is the subject matter for another discourse entirely. In brief, Japan took the territory from China in the Sino-Japanese wars, then following World War II, Japan had to cede its control over Taiwan, leaving that small country in a position of relative freedom which it has fought to maintain.

China's window of opportunity to retake control was open following World War II, yet conflict in Korea did two things to stop that: the war diverted China's attention and resources elsewhere; and it increased the United States' protection toward Taiwan, which it considered to be a potential target of communist control.

China also lost over two thirds of its soldiers who were captured when those soldiers elected not to be repatriated, instead choosing to go to Taiwan, where they were greeted as anti-communist heroes.

The Korean War significantly damaged relations between the Soviet Union and China.

The Soviet Union Has Mixed Results

Although the Soviet Union never officially entered into the Korean conflict, its influence ruled decision making of the parties consistently throughout. The Soviet Union had agreed to side with China in the event of a war. It had provided finances, military supplies and weapons, and information to China and North Korea. North Korea as a government was created by Soviet influence. The mere presence of the Soviet Union served as enough of a threat to mandate behavior from the countries of the United Nations, which feared provoking the giant super power.

With these considerable investments in place, the resulting stalemate, in which neither side managed to gain any significant victory, proved to be a politically embarrassing event for the Soviets. Its relationship with China was damaged; meanwhile democracies of the world united in spirit against the communist threat, strengthening resistance to Soviet control over the nations of Europe.

On the other hand, the Soviet Union was able to take advantage of the situation, not only by using it as a testing ground for weaponry and artillery, but by capturing weapons and technology from the American military, allowing it to retro-engineer a number of developments to bolster its own military. Its troops and spies gained experience. Like any military power, the Soviet Union was able to use the war as a training exercise.

Japan Makes the Best of a Bad Situation

Japan seems to be the only country to find the Korean War directly advantageous, using its role in the conflict as a positive step toward its position as a technological power. Having been demilitarized, the country was unable to engage directly in the war. Instead, Japan was in a prime location to serve as a valuable springboard for the United States and United Nations into Korea. Japan established its importance as a supporting force, and rapidly geared its manufacturing toward supporting the United Nations war effort. American forces relied on Japan for their voluminous supply needs, and it stands to reason that production on the spot in Japan was a far superior option to waiting for supplies to come from the United States or even Europe. In the first year of the conflict, manufacturing in Japan increased by 50 percent. The country's rise as a technological power has continued since that time.

Conclusion -
or Lack Thereof

Why was the Korean War considered the "Forgotten War," in the United States? At the time of the war, the United States was suffering from what might simply be called "overload." World War II had ended only five years earlier, and the United States underwent pervasive social adjustment both during and after. Citizens of the United States had generally rallied around the cause of that War, making sacrifices as needed and following the drama of the conflict.

Five years later, another war breaking out failed to generate much in the way of patriotic enthusiasm. The Cold War was harder to pinpoint, and while Americans felt a deep distrust of the idea of Communism or the "Reds," it was difficult to direct these concerns toward the happenings in a little Asian country about which the public knew very little. The Red Scare was much more frightening when it was thought to be menacing European nations, with which the Americans more closely identified, or when it was a nebulous scourge that could be slipping through our very society.

If anything, the end of the Korean War and its lack of any definite resolution only increased the concerns of the American people about the "Red Menace" of communism. We had been unable to stop it even in a small country like North Korea. The Red Scare gained momentum and continued to permeate our society for another few years. Yet even after blacklisting and McCarthyism died down, our fears of the Soviet Union, China, and North Korea remained and the Cold War only grew in scope.

The Korean War also established a Cold War trope called the "proxy war," meaning that two or more super powers (i.e., the United States, the Soviet Union, China) can fight a war against one another in a separate country altogether; subsequent wars in Afghanistan and Vietnam have been proxy wars. It isn't hard to imagine the resentment and permanent damage that is caused by this disregard, as super powers ravage the people and land of (in all three cases) a smaller and less affluent nation to serve as a battleground for their disputes. Korea was left in ruins by the Korean War, all of its major cities destroyed and its roads, bridges and infrastructure bombed into uselessness. The United States has sent aid to South Korea to offset financial damage; whether one believes that financial compensation erases the damage done is a personal matter.

Conflict continued through the subsequent decades in Korea, with the North and South engaging in a "Frozen War." While few shots were fired across the DMZ, their ideologies and governments remained at irreconcilable odds.

If not outright animosity, suspicion at least continues between the nations of North and South Korea, with occasional preludes to officially entering into a peace treaty or taking other steps toward unification; as is the case with many an ideological argument, a great deal of talking is done without much subsequent action.

Continually North Korean withdraws from negotiations and summits citing violations of the Armistice or the failure of the United States to comply with its standards of behavior. It is true that the United States broke the armistice as early as 1956, when it announced plans to introduce atomic weapons into South Korea, in direct violation of the Armistice's agreement that no new weapons be introduced to the countries by either side. Meanwhile in the years that followed, South Korea named well over

200 instances when North Korea violated the terms of the armistice. Investigation of these instances seldom leads to concrete answers and an uneasy truce continues to exist. China signed a peace agreement with South Korea in 1992, and withdrew from the Armistice Committee in 1994. Now only North Korea and the United Nations remain a part of the Armistice Committee.

Beginning in 2018, efforts began to reduce tensions in the DMZ, which included:

The Destruction of approximately 22 front-line guard posts along the DMZ, followed by the withdrawal of military personnel from those areas. For the most part, this was accomplished. Eventually only 20 guard posts were dismantled. Two remain on opposite sides of the border.

Military engineers spent twenty days removing landmines from the Joint Security Area and Arrowhead Hill (which then allowed the resumption of railroad transportation in the zone - South Korea in fact conducts DMZ-themed train tours)

Surveys are now allowed, to lay the foundation for new roads and railways to be built between the two nations.

Currently there are efforts between the two nations to "end" the war, for in 2018 the leaders of both nations (Moon Jae-in, President of The Republic of Korea, and Kim Jong-un, Chairman of the Democratic People's Republic of Korea) signed the Panmunjom Declaration, an announcement that they will try to put an end to the conflict between their nations, working instead toward a denuclearized and united Korean peninsula.

As recently as June 30, 2019, President Donald Trump held a summit with Northern leader Kim Jong-Un and Southern leader Moon Jae-in in the DMZ, and President Trump became the first sitting U.S. President to cross the border of North Korea. The three leaders subsequently held a meeting at the Inter-Korean House of Freedom, also in the DMZ.

In the United States, the Korean War has gained more recognition in recent decades. During the Clinton administration, the Korean War Memorial was opened in Washington D.C. where President Clinton, along with President Kim Young Sam, of the Republic of Korea, dedicated the monument on the 42nd anniversary of Korean Armistice. In hindsight, the Korean War was a game-changing conflict. This was a war that in many regrettable ways set the stage for world superpower conflicts in the decades that followed.

Is it still America's "Forgotten War," as it has often been called? As the landscape of world conflict continues, it has become necessary to look back to the Korean Conflict in order to understand the present tensions in the region. Anyone who wishes to consider themselves educated about the United States' relationships to the world's superpowers, and the small countries caught in between, must look first to the Korean War, which far too accurately represents the template for conflict in the many wars still to come.